Jesse Owens
Running into History

By the Editors of TIME For Kids
WITH ELAINE ISRAEL

Collins
An Imprint of HarperCollinsPublishers

About the Author: Elaine Israel is an editor of children's books and educational materials as well as an author. She fondly remembers her father's stories of being in Berlin in 1936 when Jesse Owens triumphed at the Olympics.

Library of Congress Cataloging-in-Publication Data is available.
ISBN 978-0-06-057620-2 (pbk.) — ISBN 978-0-06-057621-9 (trade)

2 3 4 5 6 7 8 9 10
First Edition

Photography and Illustration Credits:
Cover: photo of Jesse Owens provided by CMG Worldwide, www.jesseowens.com; cover inset: Ross Land-Getty Images; cover flap: photo of Jesse Owens provided by CMG Worldwide, www.jesseowens.com;; title page: photo provided by CMG Worldwide; contents page: photo provided by CMG Worldwide; p. iv: Hulton-Deutsch Collection/Corbis; p. 1: no credit; p. 2: CORR-AFP-Getty Images; p. 3: Hulton Archives/Getty Images; p. 4: Eudora Welty-Corbis; p. 5: Corbis; p. 6: Bettmann-Corbis; p. 7: General Research and Reference Division, Schomburg Center for Research in Black Culture, The New York Public Library; p. 8: Cleveland Public Library Photographic Collection; p. 9: courtesy the Ohio State University Archives; p. 10: Bettmann-Corbis; p. 11: Bettmann-Corbis; p. 12: The New York Times Co.-Getty Images; p. 13: Bettmann-Corbis; p. 14: Photography Collection, Miriam and Ira D. Wallach Division of Art, Prints and Photographs, The New York Public Library; p. 15: Corbis; p. 16: Bettmann-Corbis; p. 17: Bettmann-Corbis; p. 18: Fox Photos-Getty Images; p. 19 (top): courtesy The Jesse Owens Memorial Park & Museum; p. 19 (bottom): Bettmann-Corbis; p. 20 (top): Bettmann-Corbis; p. 20 (middle): Bettmann-Corbis; p. 20 (bottom): Bettmann-Corbis; p. 21 (top): Bettmann-Corbis; p. 21 (bottom): Rykoff Collection-Corbis; p. 22: Hulton-Deutsch Collection-Corbis; p. 23: AP Photo; p. 24: Bettmann-Corbis; p. 25: Bettmann-Corbis; p. 26: Bettmann-Corbis; p. 27 (top): Bettmann-Corbis; p. 27 (bottom): Bettmann-Corbis; p. 28 (top): Bettmann-Corbis; p. 28 (bottom): Bettmann-Corbis; p. 29: Bettmann-Corbis; p. 30: Bettmann-Corbis; p. 31: Hulton Archive-Getty Images; p. 32: AP Photo; p. 33: Bettmann-Corbis; p. 34 (left): Terry O'Neill-Hulton Archive-Getty Images; p. 34 (right): Bettmann-Corbis; p. 35 (top): courtesy the Ohio State University Archives; p. 35 (bottom): AFP-Getty Images; p. 36: courtesy the Ohio State University Archives; p. 37: Corbis; p. 38: AP Photo; p. 39: Jerry Cooke-Corbis; p. 40 (top): courtesy the Ohio State University Archives; p. 40 (bottom): Aarron Walter; p. 41: Bettmann-Corbis; p. 42: Jerry Lampen—Reuters/Corbis; p. 43: (top): Duomo/Corbis; p. 43 (bottom): Richard T. Nowitz—Corbis; p. 44 (top): Corbis; p. 44 (middle): Bettmann-Corbis; p. 44 (middle): Bettmann-Corbis; p. 44 (bottom): Bettmann-Corbis; chapter openers: © IOC-Olympic Museum Collection

Acknowledgments:
For TIME FOR KIDS: Art Director: ShapiroDesign; Photography Editor: Jon Protas

 Find out more at www.timeforkids.com/bio/owens

CONTENTS

". . . the only victory that counts is the one over yourself."

—JESSE OWENS

◄ **UP, UP, AND AWAY!** Jesse Owens practices a long jump before the Olympic Games.

CHAPTER 1

The Gold
STANDARD

Jesse Owens loved to run. As a young boy, he ran through cotton fields in Alabama. As a teenager, he ran on city streets in Ohio. And now came the moment that the twenty-two-year-old athlete had been training for—the Olympic Summer Games.

In 1936 the Games were held in Berlin, Germany. Adolf Hitler, Germany's leader, was the head of the Nazi party. The Nazis hated blacks, Jews, and others who were not "pure" Germans. To Hitler, the Games would prove that blond-haired, blue-eyed German athletes were supermen and superwomen. Being a black American, Jesse Owens was not part of the Nazis'

▶ **THIS IS** a souvenir of the 1936 Olympic Summer Games.

"master race." But he did not care. He was only thinking about running, jumping—and winning.

A light rain was falling during Jesse's first big race for a medal, the 100-meter run. The dirt track was uneven and messy. But from the starting shot, Jesse seemed to fly. The speed of his graceful high step set him apart as he focused on reaching the finish line. Then, just as the race neared its end, teammate Ralph Metcalfe began to catch up. The crowd cheered on the racers as Jesse sprinted ahead. He tied the record of 10.3 seconds and won the race by a comfortable one meter (3.3 feet). The gold medal was his.

Over the next week, Jesse set three new world records—in the broad jump, the 200-meter run, and the 400-meter relay. He became the first American track-and-field star to win four gold medals at a single Olympics. According to a reporter who witnessed the scene, Hitler, who was sitting down, gave "a friendly little Nazi salute" but didn't stand

◄ GERMAN ATHLETE Lutz Long (left) and Jesse became friends at the Olympics.

up and cheer. Lutz Long, a famous German broad-jumper, congratulated the man who beat him. A German filmmaker recording the Olympics for Hitler focused her camera on Jesse. Children in Berlin followed the American athlete, chanting his name. Jesse's warm smile became a familiar sight in newspapers and to his fans.

The grandson of former slaves, Jesse Owens was now famous and admired around the world. Though he would never brag, he was very proud of himself. Few people realized how hard his journey to the championship had been—a journey that began twenty-two years before, in a shack in Alabama.

CHAPTER 2

XI
OLYMPIADE
BERLIN
1936

Working the
LAND

When James Cleveland Owens was young, it didn't seem that he would ever go very far. The youngest child of Mary (called Emma) and Henry Owens, he was born on September 12, 1913. The family lived in a drafty shack in Oakville, Alabama. As a young boy, J.C. was thin and sickly.

▼ IN THE 1920S, kids played outdoor games such as Ring Around the Rosy.

He suffered all his life from pneumonia, a serious lung disease. To protect his chest, his parents wrapped him in cotton animal-feed bags. At night J.C. slept in front of the stove to stay warm.

When J.C. was six years old, he joined his six brothers and three sisters picking cotton. The Owens family were sharecroppers. They lived on someone else's property and used the owner's tools and machinery

▲ SHARECROPPERS worked long, hard hours picking cotton from sunrise to sunset.

to work the land. The owner received half the season's crop as payment. Sharecroppers worked in the sizzling heat, from sunrise to sunset in the spring and summer. Work hours were even longer during the fall harvesting season. The children could go to school only when they weren't needed in the fields.

THE GREAT MIGRATION

From 1910 to 1930, more than one million blacks left the South for northern cities. They fled prejudice and they left fields overrun by the boll weevil, which destroyed the cotton crop, leaving many people out of work.

In Chicago, Detroit, New York City, and Cleveland, black southerners found factory jobs and better lives. But even in the North, black men and women were still paid less than whites. This meant both parents had to work to support their family. More than 85 percent of black women worked. (Only 30 percent of white women born in the U.S. held jobs.)

Life in the North was tough. Yet it held hope for the migrants' children. The journey, said one black minister, was not "the end of a struggle but only its beginning."

J.C. was busy, but he still found time to swim, fish, and run. "I always loved running," he recalled later in life. "I loved it because it was something you could do all by yourself, under your own power. You could go in any direction ... seeking new sights just on the strength of your own feet and the courage of your lungs."

A Better Life

Lillie, one of J.C.'s sisters, had moved north to Cleveland, Ohio. She wrote letters to her parents about her life there. She said Cleveland had factories and mills where her father and older brothers could find work. It had schools where J.C. could get a full-time education. Lillie urged her parents to leave the town of Oakville and join her.

The Owens family had deep roots in northern Alabama. They had family and friends there, and a church that they went to every Sunday. Henry was frightened of going to a big city. But Emma saw only endless poverty ahead for her children if they didn't take the chance and leave. So in 1922 the family went to join Lillie in Ohio. Standing on the tiny train platform, J.C. asked, "Where's the train gonna take us, Momma?" She replied, "It's gonna take us to a better life."

▼ BAPTIST CHURCHES in the South were gathering places for African Americans.

CHAPTER 3

On the Right
TRACK

In Cleveland the family rented a house in a poor part of town. Henry and his older sons worked in the steel mills. Emma and her girls cleaned other people's homes and took in

▲ JESSE'S father and brothers worked in Cleveland's smoky steel mills.

laundry. Still, life was better than it had been in Oakville. Sometimes there was even money for a few extras, like new shoes and nicer furniture.

Now, instead of working in the fields, J.C. was able to go to school. On his first day at Bolton

Elementary, J.C.'s first-grade teacher misheard him when she asked for his name. To her, it sounded like "Jesse." And so it was Jesse forever after that.

Jesse had hardly learned to read and write in Alabama, and he didn't improve much during his years at Bolton. After graduating from Bolton, Jesse went to Fairmount Junior High School. Since most of its students were poor, the school knew that many would not be able to go on to college. So Fairmount prepared its students to get jobs when they graduated. Fairmount offered mostly vocational classes, such as training to work with machines. These classes didn't help Jesse to become a stronger student.

▲ CHARLES RILEY saw right away that Jesse had a talent for running.

At Fairmount Jesse met Charles Riley, the school athletics coach. Riley had seen Jesse run near the school and believed that this skinny kid had a great future as a runner. Even though Fairmount didn't have a track team, Riley decided to help Jesse improve his running technique. Riley became like a second father to Jesse. Riley was liked by everyone. This was the way Jesse wanted to be.

"Dancing on Hot Coals"

As a teen, Jesse had to earn money to help his family. He delivered groceries and worked in a shoe repair shop after school. The only time left for running was before dawn. Every morning Jesse ran through an alley near school. Coach Riley would be waiting there with a hot breakfast. Jesse said that Coach Riley taught him to run as if he was "dancing on hot coals." That was the start of Jesse's famous high-stepping style.

◀CHARLIE PADDOCK (left) gets ready to run a race. He became a hero to Jesse.

One day the coach introduced Jesse to Charlie Paddock. This famous runner had won three Olympic medals in 1920 and one in 1924. Paddock became Jesse's hero. From the moment they met, Jesse dreamed of going to the Olympics.

But it soon seemed as if Jesse's Olympic hopes would have to be forgotten. In 1929 terrible economic problems hit the United States. These hard times were called the Great Depression. One out of every four working Americans lost their jobs. Many people lost their homes and went hungry. Jesse's brothers lost their jobs. Jesse and his sisters earned little money. Even

GREAT DEPRESSION

The 1920s had been a booming time. Many people put their money in stocks, which meant they owned shares of a company.

In 1929 the prices of stocks sold on the stock market fell. All those shares were now worth very little.

Another reason for the Great Depression was that people couldn't pay back loans to banks. That caused the banks to close. The banks couldn't give back the money people had been saving. Over the next three years, businesses shut down. People lost their jobs, homes, and life savings.

▲ **WINNING** high school track meets was easy for Jesse. He won seventy-five of the seventy-nine races he ran at East Tech.

worse, Henry Owens was hit by a taxi and broke his leg. He could never work again.

After Fairmount Jesse went to Cleveland East Technical High School, where he joined the track team and continued to train with Coach Riley. Some of Jesse's family wanted him to leave school and look for a full-time job. Emma agreed with the coach that Jesse showed athletic promise. She made Jesse stay in school and keep on running.

Jesse decided to try out for the 1932 Olympic

Games in Los Angeles, California. At the Olympic trials, he soon learned that he wasn't ready. The pressure got to him. Jesse became nervous and lost three important races. For the first time, he learned what it was like to face Olympic-level athletes. They were more powerful, older, and more experienced than the high school athletes Jesse had competed against before.

Jesse kept training, breaking some world records and tying others. He was proud to be elected captain of the East Tech track team. When he ran or jumped, Jesse always looked straight ahead, paying no attention to the cheers around him. One newspaper called him "the one-man team." To honor him, Cleveland threw a parade after his last meet. It was an event Jesse would never forget.

▶ THE WINGS OF MERCURY, messenger of the gods, were the East Tech track team symbol.

CHAPTER 4

Jesse Goes to
COLLEGE

In 1933 teenage Jesse faced some grown-up problems. He got his sixteen-year-old girlfriend, Ruth Solomon, pregnant. Ruth's parents were angry and wouldn't let her see Jesse. After their daughter, Gloria Shirley, was born, Ruth went to work at a beauty parlor and lived with her parents. When Gloria was a few months old, Ruth's dad let Jesse visit.

Meanwhile, Jesse was trying to decide which college to attend. Several schools wanted him for his track-and-field skills, which would help them win meets. Jesse chose Ohio State University (OSU) in Columbus, the state capital. This upset some of Jesse's

▶ JESSE WENT TO OHIO STATE UNIVERSITY in Columbus. He was one of a few black students there.

fans. They said that OSU had a long history of badly treating its few black students. But Jesse did not change his mind.

OSU wanted him to start in the fall of 1933, but Jesse still had to finish some high school courses. The university helped Jesse take a special test so he could get his diploma from East Tech. Jesse became the first in his family to finish high school. The university also helped him find jobs that would pay his bills, yet still leave time for training. In one

such job, Jesse worked as an elevator man at night in the back of the state capitol. (Whites ran the front elevators during the day.)

▲ SIGNS such as this one in Detroit, Michigan, were not uncommon—even in the North.

In the 1930s, when the OSU track team traveled, the black athletes had to sleep and eat in places that were set apart for blacks only. In some towns, they were shut out of meets because of their skin color. This was especially true in the South. Southern states had strict laws that kept blacks and whites separate, or segregated. Blacks had to sit in the back of buses or stand, even if there were seats in the front. Black students went to separate and poorly equipped schools.

Northern states did not have segregation laws, yet blacks there still faced plenty of prejudice. Jesse was not welcome to live on the grounds of OSU. He could not eat at restaurants near the school. Only one shabby movie theater in town admitted blacks.

For much of his life, Jesse looked only at the bright side of things. Maybe this was how he protected himself. Jesse was certainly treated badly on some of his trips for OSU, but he rarely talked about the prejudice he had suffered. Everyone he met liked him, and that seemed to be enough.

His Finest Day

The week before attending a Big Ten Conference championship in Ann Arbor, Michigan, Jesse hurt his back. But he said he was

JESSE sets a new world record in the 220-yard dash at the Big Ten meet.

well enough to compete . . . and compete he did!
Years later, Jesse would remember that day—
May 25, 1935—calling it the finest day of his life.

In the long jump, he soared 26 feet, $8\frac{1}{2}$ inches
and broke the world record by almost 6 inches.
He ran the 220-yard dash in 20.3 seconds—
$\frac{3}{10}$ of a second better than the old record. He
ran the 220-yard low hurdles in 22.6 seconds,
setting another record.
In all, Jesse Owens
broke five world track-
and-field records and
tied a sixth—all in
forty-five minutes. He
was the first athlete
to break that many
records in one day.

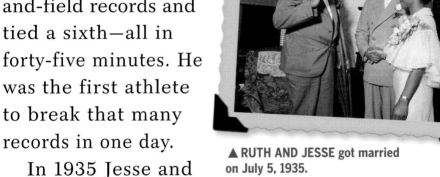

▲ **RUTH AND JESSE** got married
on July 5, 1935.

In 1935 Jesse and
Ruth were married
in the Solomons' living room. But, as Ruth was
to discover, Jesse would not stay in one place for
long. He was always on his way somewhere else.

Years later, Jesse said "being in motion was
always what made me tick. It's what made running
so natural to me. . . . I hated to sit or to stand still."

CHAPTER 5

Let the Games
BEGIN

B y 1936 the world was slowly becoming aware of the cruel way the Nazis were treating Jews and others in Germany. Adolf Hitler was taking away people's rights—having them killed or jailed as he prepared to start a war. As a result, some Americans didn't want their Olympic team to go to the Berlin games. The head of the American Olympic Committee, a supporter of the Nazis, went to Germany to see the situation for himself. He reported that all was well. "I have not heard of anything to indicate discrimination of any race or religion," he said. The United States would take part.

▶ ADOLF HITLER, the German dictator, gives a Nazi salute.

However, taking part in the Olympics was not a sure thing for any athlete, not even Jesse. First, he had to qualify at the trials in New York City. He did well at the first tryout, and again at the semifinals. The finals came a week later—and the stadium seemed to be jinxed that day. Many seats were empty. The loudspeakers broke. A sudden thunderstorm dumped rain on the athletes. But as far as Jesse was concerned, it was a perfect day. He finished first in his events and would be going to Germany.

Just before leaving for Berlin, Jesse was invited to a sports dinner in New York City, where he met Babe Ruth, the famous baseball player. Babe advised Jesse: It's not enough to want to win. Deep down you need to know you're going to win. Jesse remembered those words as he sailed to Germany on the S.S. *Manhattan*. He knew he could win.

During the nine-day trip, Jesse kept up his training—when he wasn't seasick. He ran on the decks. At 5 feet 10 inches, he was a trim 165 pounds and

▶ JESSE DEMONSTRATES his hurdling style on board the ship taking him to the Olympics.

wanted to stay that way. Some of the other American athletes spent the journey eating and drinking. They were not in great shape when they arrived in Germany.

The Germans had heard about Jesse's fame. Nazi newspapers said black athletes were "inhuman." But some Germans were thrilled to meet Jesse. He and his teammate Ralph Metcalfe were amused by the attention they got as they explored

► RALPH METCALFE and Jesse were teammates and friends. Many Germans had never seen a black person before.

▲ AN ILLUSTRATION of an ancient Greek footrace

OLYMPIC HISTORY

The first Olympic Games were held in Olympia, Greece, around 777 B.C. Only men were allowed to take part. Events included boxing, wrestling, and chariot racing. No medals were awarded. Instead, winners received a crown of olive leaves. The Games continued for more than 1,000 years, but were cancelled in 393 A.D.

In 1894 French teacher Pierre de Coubertin wanted to bring the Games back. He believed that

► PIERRE DE COUBERTIN, founder of the modern Olympics

Berlin. People who had never seen blacks before were fascinated by the color of their skin. Crowds mobbed them and followed them everywhere.

The Games Begin

The Games began with great ceremony on August 1, 1936. Red, black, and white Nazi banners lined the streets. Inside the huge new Olympic stadium, a band played. Outside, there was a twenty-one-gun salute. The world's largest zeppelin—a blimp named the *Hindenburg*—flew overhead, pulling an Olympic flag.

▲ THE HINDENBURG flies over the Olympic stadium on opening day.

◀ A POSTCARD of the stadium in 1896

a modern Olympics with athletes from all over the world would promote peace and understanding among nations.

The modern Olympics started in Athens, Greece, in 1896. Only summer events were included. Figure skating was part of the Summer Olympics in 1908. The sport later became part of the Winter Games, which started in 1924.

The spirit of the ancient Olympics is still alive today. The Games are a source of national pride and peaceful competition. The 2008 Summer Olympics will be held in China, and billions of people will be watching it on television.

As the teams arrived, many in the stands gave the Nazi salute, stiffly stretching out their right arms. A tall, blond runner lit the Olympic flame. German boys freed doves from their cages. For a moment, the sky was dark with fluttering wings. Adolf Hitler declared the Games officially underway.

Two days later, Jesse began his runs and

▲ JESSE wins the broad jump, setting a world record.

jumps into the history books. After beating Ralph Metcalfe in the 100-meter run, he soared 26 feet, $5\frac{1}{4}$ inches in the broad jump. That was a world record that would last until 1960. In the 200-meter race, his time of 20.7 seconds broke another record. "It seems to take an eternity," Jesse said about running a race. "Yet it is all over before you can think what's happening."

After the 200-meter run, Jesse looked forward to resting. Instead, Dean Cromwell, the U.S. coach, told him that he and Ralph Metcalfe would take the places

of two other Americans in the 400-meter relay race. Those two runners, Marty Glickman and Sam Stoller, were the only Jewish members of the track-and-field team. Jesse pleaded for them and for himself. "I am tired. Let Marty and Sam run. They deserve it." Both Glickman and Stoller believed they were pulled from the race because they were Jewish. The relay team did win gold, setting a world record of 39.8 seconds that stood for twenty years. But to American fans, it was not a moment to be proud of.

The Winners

When the games were over, the Germans had won eighty-nine medals—more medals than any other country. The Americans were second with sixty-six.

Then in 1939 World War II broke out in Europe. Two years later the U.S. entered the fight. The war didn't end until 1945. The next Olympic Games were held in 1948 in London, England.

CHAPTER 6

Going
HOME

For every bright moment in Jesse's life, there seemed to be a dark cloud, too.

In Jesse's time, college and Olympic athletes were amateurs; they were not allowed to earn money for their sport. This rule was enforced by the Amateur Athletic Union (AAU). However, in 1936, the AAU was running out of cash. Their solution was to send the American Olympic team on a tour of Europe to compete against local athletes. The AAU would charge people to attend these meets. Union officials were really counting on Jesse. They knew many

◄ AAU-SPONSORED events were popular among sports fans. Here famed athlete and Olympic champion Babe Didrikson jumps a hurdle.

people would pay to see him.

But Jesse just wanted to go home. For one thing, he was broke. And he missed his family. He felt that he must take advantage of his fame and earn some money for himself before people forgot about him. It was now or never.

Jesse gave in to the AAU and visited a few countries with his teammates. He was worn out, though, and did not perform well. When the team left for Sweden, Jesse was finished. He borrowed money for the fare, boarded the *Queen Mary*, and sailed for New York.

The AAU suspended Jesse because he left before the tour was over. That meant he would never be allowed to take part in any more amateur track-and-field events. If he returned to college, as he planned to do, he would not be allowed to compete for his school either.

This news was upsetting, but Jesse was just thinking about heading home. He received a hero's welcome when his ship arrived in New York City. His parents

▶ JESSE was greeted with kisses from his mother (left) and wife, Ruth, when he came back from Europe.

▲ CLEVELAND held a parade for Jesse after he came home.

and Ruth were there to greet him. New York and Cleveland both held parades in his honor.

Home Again

Jesse was thrilled by all the attention he received when he returned home. But he was sad, too. Years later, he said, "After I came home . . . with my four medals, it became increasingly apparent that everyone was going to slap me on the back. . . . But no one was going to offer me a job."

At that time, black athletes were not paid to sell products for companies. They weren't picked up by professional sports teams either. Major League Baseball had no black players until Jackie Robinson joined the Brooklyn Dodgers in 1947. Black pro-football players were first hired in 1946, while black pro-basketball players finally took the court in 1950.

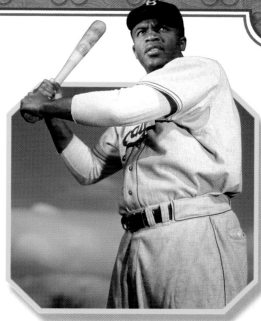

▲ JACKIE ROBINSON was the first African American player in Major League Baseball.

Jesse did get a few small jobs, however. He worked for Cleveland's parks department, cleaning a city pool's bathroom and supervising a playground. These were not the kind of jobs Jesse hoped for. But like always, he did his best.

The sports hero also traveled a lot to make money.

He was paid to give speeches—almost always about the Olympics—for Alf Landon, the Republican who ran

◄ ALF LANDON asked Jesse to campaign for him in the 1936 presidential election. Landon lost to Franklin D. Roosevelt.

for President against Franklin D. Roosevelt. (Landon badly lost the election in 1936.) Then Jesse went to Cuba, where he was supposed to race against the fastest runner on the island, Conrado Rodrigues. But the AAU warned Rodrigues that he would be banned if he took part in the race. So Jesse agreed to race

▲ JESSE raced a horse and won!

against a horse instead. Jesse won the race, but his fans were angry that he had been forced to do it. Not wanting to upset anyone, Jesse just made light of the situation.

For the rest of his life, Jesse held many different kinds of jobs. He loved meeting people. He led a nightclub orchestra once and coached black basketball and baseball teams. Jesse opened a group of dry cleaning stores, but his partners were dishonest and the chain went broke. Jesse's string of bad luck continued

▶ FOR A TIME, Jesse was a partner in a chain of drive-thru dry cleaners.

when, in 1940, his mother and then his father died.

That year Jesse decided to return to Ohio State University. Jesse and Ruth moved to Columbus with their two young daughters, Marlene and Beverly. To support his growing family and pay for college, Jesse opened a new dry cleaning store and became an assistant trainer with the OSU track team. OSU overlooked some school rules for him, but he still could not keep up with his studies. The next year he dropped out of school for good.

Jesse went to work for the Ford Motor Company in Detroit, Michigan. The factory, which once made cars, was now making materials for World War II. Because Jesse was helping the war effort, he did not have to serve in the U.S. armed forces. Jesse served as the link between Ford officials and the black employees hired to work on the assembly lines. The job lasted until 1945, when the new head of Ford changed its management system. Once again, Jesse went on the road.

▲ AFTER WORLD WAR II, Ford started to produce cars again on its assembly lines.

CHAPTER 7

The Traveling MAN

Among Jesse's happiest times were the six months he spent with the Harlem Globetrotters in 1948 and 1949. Though not part of a professional league, this black basketball team played a great game. They also clowned around and made audiences laugh. Jesse didn't play basketball with the team; instead, he greeted fans

◀ THE HARLEM GLOBETROTTERS were talented basketball players.

and gave autographs. People never tired of his stories about the 1936 Olympic Games.

Another highlight came in 1950, when the Associated Press named Jesse "the greatest track athlete of the past half century." At the dinner honoring him, one speaker said that Jesse "had won the heart of America." Jesse was very proud of that. He may not have been very successful in business, but he was able to support his wife and children. Accepting the award, Jesse spoke of his journey from poverty to success,

▲ JESSE proudly shows off some of his medals. He continued to be honored long after the 1936 Olympics.

and about living the "American dream." He said, "In America, anyone can become somebody. . . . It happened to me, and I believe it can happen to anybody in one way or another."

▲ JESSE met with thousands of people on trips to Asia. On a stop in the Philippines, he showed kids the starting position for racing.

Helping the U.S.

When World War II ended, the Cold War began. It was fought mainly with ideas and strong words rather than guns. The United States and other democracies, nations whose governments are freely elected by their citizens, were on one side. The nations that made up the Soviet Union were on the other. They believed in a system of government called Communism. There were no free elections. The government decided what your job would be and where you would go to school.

President Dwight D. Eisenhower was a great fan of Jesse's. In 1955 he asked Jesse to visit several nations whose support was needed to fight Communism. Jesse's trip for the U.S. Department of State lasted more than three months. He spoke to school groups in India, Malaysia, and the Philippines. Along the way, he made many

Mystery PERSON

CLUE 1: I was born on June 23, 1940, in Clarksville, Tennessee. When I was four years old, I became very ill. I couldn't use my left leg. After years of hospital treatments, my leg got better.

CLUE 2: When I was thirteen, I made the all-state basketball team. I also liked running and joined my college track team.

CLUE 3: I won a bronze medal in the relay at the Olympic Games in 1956. In 1960 I became the first American woman to win three medals in one Olympics. After that, some people called me "the Jesse Owens of women's track-and-field."

Who am I?

Fast Facts

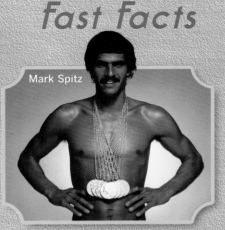

Mark Spitz

PERSONAL BESTS

Here's a look at some Olympic highlights.

1912 Jim Thorpe, an American Indian, won both the decathlon (ten track-and-field events) and pentathlon (five events).

1948 Fanny Blankers-Koen, a Dutch runner, was the first woman to win three individual gold medals.

1960 Abebe Bikila, a barefoot marathon runner from Ethiopia, became the first black African to win a gold medal. In 1964 he won again.

1972 Swimmer Mark Spitz of the U.S. won seven gold medals at a single Olympics.

2000 Steven Redgrave, a rower from Britain, was the first athlete to win gold medals in five straight Olympics.

▲ PRESIDENT DWIGHT EISENHOWER knew Jesse would be an excellent goodwill ambassador for the U.S.

friends for the United States. Later he did the same in Africa.

The next year, Jesse was on the go again—this time to speak at the 1956 Olympic Games in Melbourne, Australia. Jesse spoke about his faith in the United States and of the need to work hard. He most liked talking to young people and

urged them to stay out of trouble by taking part in sports.

Jesse enjoyed being treated as a hero. But as he watched the 1956 American team break his record in the 400-meter relay, he realized that many younger athletes were passing him by. Four years later, at the Games in Rome, Italy, Jesse's long jump record was broken by American Ralph Boston. This was hard for Jesse to watch. But he knew he would always hold an important place in sports history.

▶ RALPH BOSTON broke Jesse's long jump record in 1960.

CHAPTER 8

The Home
STRETCH

For the rest of his life, Jesse enjoyed being a celebrity. In 1960 he was honored on *This Is Your Life*, a TV show that surprised famous people by bringing together their family and friends. One of the guests was Charles Riley, Jesse's former coach. The two men had been out of touch since 1946. Now eighty-two and in poor health, Coach Riley had

◄ IN 1960 Jesse was the guest on a popular television show where people from his past honored him.

traveled to California from his home in Florida to honor Jesse. Riley died later that year.

The 1960s were a time of great change in the United States. Black people marched and protested, demanding equal rights. But speaking out against prejudice was not Jesse's way. He disagreed with the younger black men and women who called for violence and a hatred of white people.

Troubled Times

Jesse never gave up believing that anyone who tried hard enough could succeed. Again and again, he urged people to work hard and help themselves rather than depend on the government for support. He agreed with the ideas of the civil rights leader Martin Luther King Jr. but never joined his nonviolence movement.

▲ MARTIN LUTHER KING JR. led the civil rights movement.

In 1968 black athletes talked of staying away from the Olympics in Mexico City. They wanted to boycott as a protest against discrimination in the

United States. In the end, the athletes took part in the Games, but some showed their anger in other ways. As Tommie Smith and John Carlos stood on the awards platform, each raised a gloved fist in the air as a protest against discrimination.

▼ AS A PROTEST against discrimination, some black athletes raised their fists at the 1968 Olympics.

U.S. Olympic officials wanted to suspend the two men. Jesse thought he might get the two runners to apologize. He didn't want them to be banned from amateur sports as he had been. Later, when he spoke to the team in the locker room, no one wanted to listen to him. The athletes said Jesse was behind the times. Neither the runners nor the officials would give in. In the end, both Smith and Carlos were suspended from the team.

Finally Jesse came to realize what a terrible rage

young black people had within them. He knew that his smile and his words could not soften their feelings, nor the pain and suffering of so many black Americans. He recognized the great gap between his experience and old-fashioned ideas and those of younger people. "Probably I haven't changed enough," he said, "but at least I can say . . . I'm still changing."

Never Forgotten

After the 1968 Olympics, Jesse still remained a popular hero to many. In order to talk about his life, he helped write a book called *I Have Changed.* In it he listed his schedule for a week in 1971. Just reading the list of speeches and appearances could make most people tired. But Jesse was never still.

Jesse and Ruth decided to move to Scottsdale, Arizona, where life would be more quiet and comfortable. In early 1979 he came down again with pneumonia, the lung disease that he had suffered from throughout his life. It didn't help that he had been a smoker.

▶ JESSE AND RUTH moved to Arizona for his health.

He almost collapsed during a speech later that year. It turned out that Jesse had lung cancer.

Jesse Owens died on March 31, 1980. Ruth was at his side. Jesse believed people should be honored during their lifetimes, not afterward. But the tributes poured in anyway. Ohio State University named a plaza for him. His Cleveland high school planted a grove of trees in his memory. The Jesse Owens Memorial Park, including a museum, was built in Oakville, Alabama, near his childhood home. Even in Germany, a street

leading to the old Olympic stadium was named after Jesse.

In *I Have Changed*, Jesse had written, "Life is a marathon—a long, long, long-distance race over hills and through valleys. . . . It's how you run that marathon, not how soon you get to the finish line, that matters."

Jesse inspired people—especially young people around the world—to care about sports. His decency and gentleness won people's hearts.

Many athletes have set Olympic records, but few are remembered with as much affection and respect as Jesse Owens. The world's fastest man crossed life's finish line as a true American hero.

► IN 1951 Jesse visited the old Berlin Olympic stadium, where he looked at a plaque of 1936 winners. His name tops the list.

Talking About
JESSE

▲ MICHAEL JOHNSON

Michael Johnson is the holder of five Olympic gold medals in the 200-meter and 400-meter races. TIME FOR KIDS editor Kathryn Satterfield spoke with Michael Johnson about Jesse Owens.

Q: *How did Jesse Owens's performance at the 1936 Olympic Games change the world of track-and-field in the U.S. and abroad?*
A: His outstanding performances, plus the fact that he won gold medals in four events at the Olympic Games against the best in the world, redefined the limits of what was thought to be humanly possible.

Q: *How did Owens's career help shape the careers of African American athletes who followed in his strides?*
A: After representing America with the greatest performance in the history of the Olympics, he came

back to America and was treated as a second-class citizen. His effort to continue to show class and dignity shamed America, and his example paved the way for all other African American athletes.

Q: *What about his legacy do you find most inspiring?*
A: He followed in no one's footsteps and made sports history, both as a track-and-field star and as an African American. And he accomplished what he set out to achieve in the face of incredible doubt and unimaginable pressure, all because he believed in himself.

Q: *What can young track-and-field athletes learn from Owens's example?*
A: He was known as the greatest athlete in the world but remained remarkably humble and always carried himself with class and dignity. There's a lesson in there for all of us.

Jesse Owens's
KEY DATES

1913 Born on September 12 in Oakville, Alabama

1917
U.S. enters
World War I.

1922 Moves with family to Cleveland, Ohio

1927 Meets Coach Charles Riley at Fairmount Junior High School

1933 Enters Ohio State University

1935 Breaks five world records and ties a sixth at Big Ten Championship meet

1936 Wins four gold medals at the Olympic Games in Berlin

1950 Begins travels for the U.S. Department of State

The helicopter is invented.

1968 Tries to get black athletes to apologize at the Olympic Games in Mexico City

1968
Martin Luther King Jr. killed.

1980 Dies on March 31 in Tucson, Arizona